Mindful
COLOURING FOR KIDS

Buster Books

Illustrated by Sarah Wade
and Jane Ryder-Gray

Written and edited by Josephine Southon
Cover designed by Angie Allison
Designed by Zoe Bradley

First published in Great Britain in 2021 by Buster Books, an imprint of
Michael O'Mara Books Limited, 9 Lion Yard, Tremadoc Road, London SW4 7NQ

W www.mombooks.com/buster   f Buster Books   🐦 @BusterBooks   📷 @buster_books

ISBN: 978-1-78055-765-6

1 3 5 7 9 10 8 6 4 2

This book was printed in October 2021 by Leo Paper Products Ltd,
Heshan Astros Printing Limited, Xuantan Temple Industrial Zone,
Gulao Town, Heshan City, Guangdong Province, China.

FSC
www.fsc.org
MIX
Paper from
responsible sources
FSC® C020056

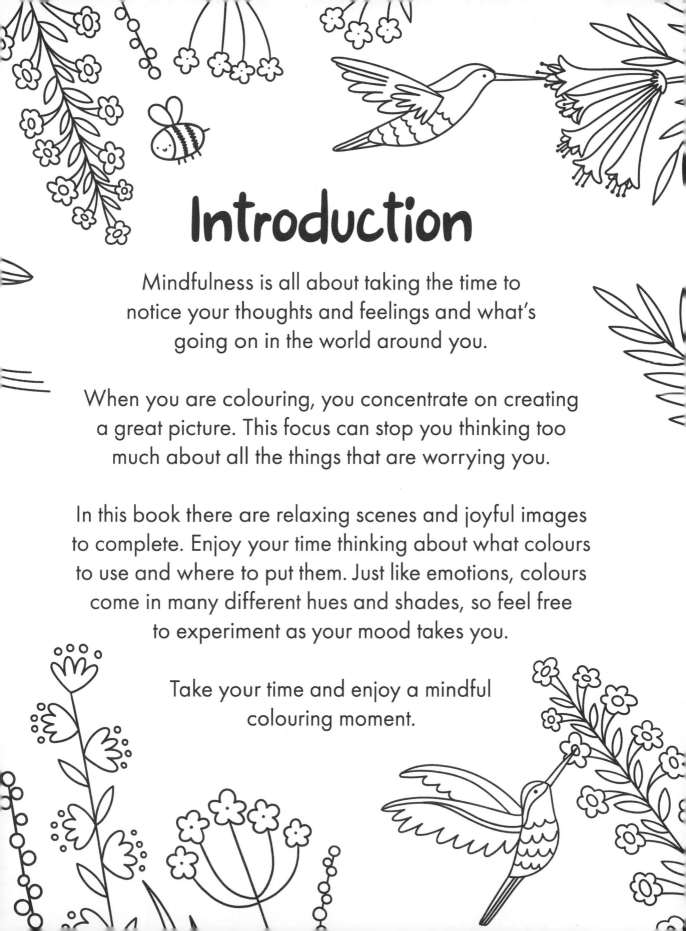

Introduction

Mindfulness is all about taking the time to notice your thoughts and feelings and what's going on in the world around you.

When you are colouring, you concentrate on creating a great picture. This focus can stop you thinking too much about all the things that are worrying you.

In this book there are relaxing scenes and joyful images to complete. Enjoy your time thinking about what colours to use and where to put them. Just like emotions, colours come in many different hues and shades, so feel free to experiment as your mood takes you.

Take your time and enjoy a mindful colouring moment.

Lean In

Begin by noticing which colours you feel most drawn to, just like a sunflower leaning to face the sun's rays or a bee making its way to the perfect flower.

Focus

Focussing on one thing at a time helps
to calm the mind. Notice how distractions
seem to melt away when you're busy
colouring this shoal of fish.

Notice Your Mood

Chameleons change colour to reflect their moods. You have a huge kaleidoscope of ever-changing emotions. What colours would you use to describe your mood in this moment?

Let the Storm Pass

Emotions such as sadness and anger can batter us like stormy seas. Remember: strong feelings, just like storms, always pass. The sun will break through the clouds again.

Seek Out Comfort

What do you turn to when you feel
scared or upset? Think of the people,
places and things that have brought you
comfort in hard times – maybe it's curling
up next to your pet, or cosying up with
a big mug of hot chocolate.

Slow Down

Do you sometimes feel like
your thoughts are racing past, or
your body is full of jittery energy?

Try being more like a sloth. Moving at
a slower pace might help you notice
interesting things around you that you
otherwise would have missed.

Meditate

Meditation can help you take a step back from the busy world around you. By sitting in a comfortable, quiet place and focussing on taking deep breaths for 5–10 minutes, you can take a break from your racing thoughts.

Listen

Notice the sounds around you as you colour these pages. Are there birds singing in the trees? Can you hear the leaves rustling in the breeze?

See, Smell, Taste

The world is full of wonderful things
that can pass us by if our senses
are not tuned into them.

Take a big sniff! Notice the smells
and savour the tastes next time
you have a bite to eat.

Take a Deep Breath

Concentrating on your breathing is a superpower that you can use whenever you're feeling upset or stressed.

Take a deep breath. Breathe out, and imagine those worries floating away like leaves dancing on the breeze.

Let it Go

When you have lots of thoughts
and worries rushing around in your
head, it can be difficult to focus.

Take each one in turn and let them
fly from your mind. It can help you
feel calmer and happier.

Connection

Healthy relationships make us feel good because we know we belong to something special.

Opening up to friends and family when you are feeling sad will help you feel less alone and bring you closer to the people who love you.

Kindness

Giving to others lets them know you care,
and it can make you feel good about yourself.
Giving does not have to be about gifts. Small
acts and words of kindness towards friends,
family and people in need go a long way.

The Power of Sleep

Have you ever noticed that you get more easily upset or frustrated when you're tired? Sleep is as important for your mind and body as eating, drinking and breathing.

Get Outdoors

When your body is active your brain
releases chemicals that make you feel happy.
Breathing in the fresh air can help to slow your
racing heart and clear your mind of worries.

You may find that going for a walk in
a park eases away your troubles.